A Child's Prayers

illustrated by Angela Jarecki

Inchworm
PRESS
New York™

Text copyright © 1997 Inchworm Press, an imprint of GT Publishing Corporation.
Illustrations © 1997 Angela Jarecki. All rights reserved.
No part of this book may be used or reproduced in any manner whatsoever
without written permission from the publisher. For information address
Inchworm Press, 16 East 40th Street, New York, New York 10016.

The Lord's Prayer

Our Father, who art in heaven,
hallowed be Thy name,
Thy kingdom come,
Thy will be done,
On earth as it is in heaven.
Give us this day our daily bread,
And forgive us our trespasses
as we forgive those
who trespass against us,
and lead us not into temptation,
but deliver us from evil.
Amen

Prayers for Morning

Through the night Thine angels kept
Watch around me while I slept.
Now the dark has gone away,
Lord, I thank Thee for the day.

Dear Lord, I offer thee this day
All I shall think, or do, or say.

Father in Heaven, all through the night
I have been sleeping, safe in Thy sight.
Father, I thank Thee; bless me I pray,
Bless me and keep me all through the day.

Prayers Before Meals

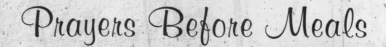

For food, and all thy gifts of love,
We give thee thanks and praise.
Look down, O Father, from above
And bless us all our days.

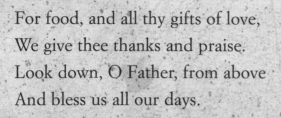

Bless us, O Lord, and these Thy gifts
Which we are about to receive
from your bounty
Through Christ our Lord.
Amen.

Come, dear Lord Jesus, be our guest,
and bless what Thou hast given us.
For Jesus' sake.
Amen.

Thou art great
And Thou art good,
And we thank Thee
For this food.
By Thy hand
Must all be fed,
And we thank Thee
For this bread.

Prayers for a Beautiful World

God made the world so broad and grand,
Filled with blessings from His hand.
He made the sky so high and blue,
and all the little children too.

Lord, make me an instrument of thy peace;
Where there is hatred, let me sow love;
Where there is injury, pardon;
Where there is discord, union;
Where there is doubt, faith;
Where there is despair, hope;
Where there is darkness, light;
Where there is sadness, joy.

St. Francis of Assisi

Prayers of Thanks

Thank you for the world so sweet,
Thank you for the food we eat.
Thank you for the birds that sing,
Thank you, God, for everything.

Thank God for rain
and the beautiful rainbow colors
and thank God for letting children
splash in the puddles.

A Child's Prayer, England

Oh, the Lord is good to me,
And so I thank the Lord,
For giving me the things I need:
The sun, the rain and the appleseed:
The Lord is good to me.

Attributed to Johnny Appleseed
(John Chapman — 1774-1845)

Prayers for Sharing

What can I give Him,
        Poor as I am?
If I were a shepherd,
        I would bring Him a lamb;
If I were a wise man,
        I would do my part;
But what can I give Him?
        Give Him my heart.
                    Christina Rossetti

God bless all those that I love;
God bless all those that love me;
God bless all those that love those that I love
And all those that love those that love me.

New England sampler

Prayers for Caring

God be in my head, and in my understanding;

God be in my eyes, and in my looking;

God be in my mouth, and in my speaking;

God be in my heart, and in my thinking;

God be at my end, and in my departing.

The Sarum Missal

May the road rise to meet you.
May the wind be always at your back.
May the sun shine warm upon your face.
May the rains fall softly upon your fields
until we meet again.
May God hold you in the hollow of his hand.

Prayers of Joy

All things bright and beautiful,
All creatures great and small,
All things wise and wonderful,
The Lord God made them all.

Each little flower that opens,
Each little bird that sings,
He made their glowing colors,
He made their tiny wings:

The purple-headed mountain,
The river running by,
The sunset and the morning,
That brightens up the sky,

The cold wind in the winter,
The pleasant summer sun,
The ripe fruits in the garden,
He made them every one.

Cecil Frances Alexander

Prayers for Bedtime

Gentle Jesus, meek and mild,
Look upon this little child;
Pity my simplicity,
Suffer me to come to Thee.
Fain I would to Thee be brought;
Dearest God, forbid it not;
Give me, dearest God, a place
In the kingdom of Thy grace.

Lord, keep us safe this night.
Secure from all our fears.
May angels guard us while we sleep,
Till morning light appears.

Cradle Hymn

Away in a manger, no crib for a bed,

The little Lord Jesus laid down his sweet head.

The stars in the bright sky looked down where he lay—

The little Lord Jesus asleep on the hay.

The cattle are lowing, the baby awakes,

But little Lord Jesus no crying he makes.

I love Thee, Lord Jesus! Look down from the sky,

And stay by my cradle till morning is nigh.

Be near me, Lord Jesus, I ask Thee to stay

Close by me forever, and love me, I pray.

Bless all the dear children, in Thy tender care,

And take us to heaven, to live with Thee there.

Martin Luther

Now I lay me down to sleep,
I pray Thee Lord, Thy child to keep:
Thy love guard me through the night
And wake me in the morning light.